DEAR, COMPANION

DEAR, COMPANION

poems by

A.E. Watkins

Dream Horse Press
California

Dream Horse Press
www.dreamhorsepress.com
Editor: J.P. Dancing Bear

Dream Horse Press
Post Office Box 2080
Aptos, California 95001-2080
U.S.A.

Watkins, A. E.
        Dear, Companion
            p.104

            ISBN 978-1-935716-21-1
            1. Poetry

10 9 8 7 6 5 4 3 2 1

First Edition

Cover: "Regeneration" by Lauren Lipinski Eisen
http://laureneisenart.com/

Table of Contents

A Legend of Loose Brick Children………...............….....…...........13

Summer
Allerton in Summer I..17
Allerton in Summer II...18
No Narrative...19
Allerton in Summer III..20
Our Apocryphal Chapter of Animals..21
Allerton in Summer IV...23
Blót..24
Narcissus and Echo, Two Voltas, a Field in Illinois......................26
Allerton in Summer V...27
The Song of the North American Chimney Swift.........................28
Allerton in Summer IV...29
Actaeon to Diana...30

Argus, All Your Eyes are Sleeping..35

Autumn
Sentences in the Picturesque..41
Allerton in Autumn I...43
Instructions for Bewilder & Amend..44
Allerton in Autumn II..45
A Manufactured Country..46
Allerton in Autumn III...48
To Callisto, The Bear...49
Allerton in Autumn IV...50
They Apply Pigeons, to Draw Vapors from the Head....................51
Allerton in Autumn V...52
The Innocent Walk Blindfold Among Burning Plow-Shares.........53
And Then One Day a Blue Sky Dims Starless...............................54

Taking the North Wind to Heart.................................59

Winter
Allerton in Winter I.................................63
Epitome.................................54
Allerton in Winter II.................................65
Writing Us in This Age and Its Climate.................................66
Allerton in Winter III.................................67
The Vacated Season.................................68
Travelling from Home.................................69
Allerton in Winter IV.................................71
Orpheus, to His Own Persephone.................................72
Allerton in Winter V.................................73
A Crosshatch of Rising Cinders, Falling Snow.................................74
Orpheus, to No One but Himself.................................75

To Alcyone, from Your Dead Husband.................................81

Spring
Allerton in Spring I.................................85
Another Evening at the Abandoned Fairground.................................87
A Process Called Night and Rain.................................88
Allerton in Spring II.................................90
To Pomona, in a House in Pomona, California.................................91
Baucis & Philemon.................................92
Allerton in Spring III.................................94
Hamlet, Indiana.................................96
The Once Wautaga Valley.................................97
Allerton in Spring IV.................................99
A Letter from Pythagoras.................................100
Allerton in Spring V.................................102

Acknowledgments.................................104

For DD

As soon as we begin to find our bearings, the landscape vanishes at a stroke like the façade of a house as we enter it.

—Walter Benjamin

For my part, I would have thought that nothing lasts for long with the same appearance. So the ages changed from gold to iron, and so the fortunes of places have altered. I have seen myself what was once firm land become sea; I have seen earth made from the waters.

—Pythagoras, according to Ovid

§

A Legend of Loose Brick Children

after W.B. Keckler

The silos as Cronos in a grainless landscape.

Humless wires as humless
rails. Vice versa.

Some crows a no-code of dots
and space, while the factory
walls stand for their past purpose.

Gone the heavy assembly-work hands of a prior century.
Still, the smokestack and dreamless morning says

total all grief

— a legend of loose brick children

throw at remaining panes.

Inside the factory, figures withered from signs,
the shatter-covered floors,

I cannot written in the windows.

Allerton in Summer

Allerton in Summer I.

Walking between two homes. A domed sky that darkened in the doorway of every puddle. And those two skies we knew, their long departures and greetings. Their dim light longing in the distance that was always between them.

That dim light. That one sky you parted with a finger. What we couldn't say but felt like. Like about us was everything haunted and nameless.

Or so rows of lamps and trees along the streets over-lapping, leaving each bulb to burn inside a ribcage of branches.

Like a language we couldn't say but dreamt in. Like the halogen glow had meant something – and those clusters of green leaves were dancing their dark cloak across it. This was how I found your eyes in a dark street's bright lights.

This is how I took their green flickering darkness.

Allerton in Summer II.

When we met, I tried endlessly to explain myself, babbling some history I wanted to spell me.

For months, I could speak only of the two-story house I was raised in, before later divorces: a suburban street out the front door, a cornfield thriving where my memory of the backyard ended.

And I told you days I would lay there in a cornrow's thinking. And I spoke of such nothing beyond that field, which gave the clouds and took them.

I'd tell you: a field can keep its past only so well, like a self-portrait caught in medias res. And I meant: a tending subject to every weather.

I said: when I was young, I believed my eyes were open gates between two horizons. My head turned out for dwelling. The world no longer beyond me.

Two homes I didn't want to tell apart any longer.

No Narrative

A paradise will foreclose once any aperture – no narrative but trees
were saying birds between them. The sun through green leaves like green

stained glass – a bright room, the birds spoken in through
a window – translating between two

weathers. Then the birds as captives or portents.
The forest and these feathered currents

coursing its chambers. And so you think
of open doors, the empty sanctuary. How their trilling

lingers the branches now rafters over several scenes –
no narrative but birds on wires humming between

poles – lining the street – front doors and an absence cut in each
tree to let the wires through: an entrance by which

a blood-thick night could pass.
The birds with beaks pulled to breasts, their small claws clasped

to a wilderness of black threads, which hums with lamp-lit
rooms and flitting.

Allerton in Summer III.

We did not live together that summer.

You lived with your parents, who were to me a far off town, but some nights you'd drive to the city that held me. And those nights I'd dream of a once empty field and some new oak that it harbored. The trunks as wide as the lampposts in the city outside our sleep.

Each tree like a conversation between two horizons, their branches abridging a distance between them. And then came

the morning drama of our parting, and the streetlamps were as thick as the oaks I had imagined. All of this I would try to explain. But nothing I said would sound like the leaf-rustle I wanted.

Our Apocryphal Chapter of Animals

When I was young, I had one summer of arrowheads.
The soil and its wealth. The first time

a girl and I agreed without speaking
that the feel of dirt in our hands, cool from beneath
the layers, was the best thing. I remember

the bird skulls she collected, the broken machines
of their wings, and how she imagined

a whole flock frozen in flight below us,
the massive rocks all over – like cold stars inside

the earth where sunless, a night of soil over
a golden age we fabled and filled

with past pets and relatives – who left us
their deaths and now lived with extinct species

we made up, believed in. But thinking this way
the ground turned mythic and hollow as a word –
my feet unsure like my tongue

telling its weight. Each secret I spent before her
like exposure and clarity imprinted on

either side of an old coin we found.

*   *   *

Those days I held her hand mainly. I held her

mind in mine and never fathomed. Like constellations
we watched and how she watched – and loved and

gloated over – my spinning; how
she renamed the constellations after,
because I could not think to do so, our apocryphal

chapter of animals. And the rest
of that summer, her glance was

the sound of arrow feathers all
over and swiftly. My body like some
creature extinct but wanting

renewal. The way she smiled to
say *mammoth*. That word flitting about

my head all summer. That word
just tore holes right through me.

Allerton in Summer IV.

A staircase in a field of tall grass. Or the ground was a vast chest of drawers, with each housing a calamity of skeleton keys, a spoil of horseshoes. Or so I found what distance tells

apart it also becomes. A home as two houses – the absence expanding between them. Then some home in the absence expanded. Then an attic door hinged to the mottled sky.

When I was young, I said, my life was small and drifting, something that would fit inside a green suitcase. And in the space of my summers, a forest refuge I fabled, the wilderness and I wandered below an arched skull blue and moonless.

Or maybe: it was a bi-polar climate I had learned to make due with. A legend that would thrive in my bedded mind, its nightlong of garden.

And maybe those nights I dreamt more tarnished handles in the ground. More drawers for me to pull clean from its soil.

And maybe the only thing worth knowing was how the river made the woods glisten and wonder. How I knew myself just like its banks. Like all I could hold was a constant departure.

Here's what I should have told you: to meet me was to find a childhood of lonely summers, of droughts and cataracts a struggling current hoarsens over. Those long nights barely choking on.

Blót

Blót: 1) A ceremony where sacrifices are made to Norse gods.
Blot: 1a) A disfiguring mark   b) Obliteration by way of correction 2) A moral
stain, fault, disgrace 3) To paint coarsely .

The boulders had looked like god-fists littering
the stubble-fields in March. Of course, those days I lived in

the suburbs with my father, but in the dream
he was dead and I would remember what was hidden

in the high tides of August.

I knew whatever my father hadn't removed was
inheritance. That field like Norse waters, my

Norse temper. Still, need got around,
vandalizing the folklore, the possible harvest.

So I took my father's unfilled clothes to make
(not an effigy) a scarecrow.

I never saw it as bearing credence to a stake.
I just knew there was empathy in twine.

I watched the sun's crown rise and tip,
spilling straw.

Some folks said if the straw man doesn't stave, it helps
to hang a couple dead ravens from his neck.

Those birds I named only when I thought to,
only when I'd remember
the rest of my life like a day of moraine,

the boulders knocking
forever at my eyes.

Narcissus and Echo, Two Voltas, A Field in Illinois

The corn stalks surprisingly tall for June: across the plain
a green-gold sea swells over the ground. High school friends yet
and never to be made, our tents, a fire on the lawn
of the old farmhouse no one would enter. How the sky darkens
like a regret slowly taking a memory. How she and I walk
our lamp down the dirt ruts of the drive; beyond the field
a steel tower like an ink sketch on black paper — two red lights
at the top flitting back and forth like a railroad signal

or echoing thrushes. And we make up a game to play
in the field, put the lamp in a tree for a beacon, a breadcrumb
of bright light, and we barrel into the gulf of corn.
Amazed in the stalk-black night, I shout out and break
in my echo's direction. I imagine our bodies as a code
of yelling and distance, as though we are finding out

ourselves — an ellipse's two points discovering their deletion
in a plain of near collisions. And when I finally stop,
the tree is nowhere to be found, but I don't
say anything. All I can see is a darkness held close –
shaped as leaves stenciled across the farther darkness –
two red dots singing the night somewhere.

Allerton in Summer V.

Down the county roads, we followed each new landscape. Found new fields and taller forests. Old towns and well-worn Midwestern cities.

It's true: the horizon was neverending, was never any closer. Like some lyric half-remembered, one line we couldn't stop thinking or singing.

Or a sun that hung always at the skyline – a landscape in a constant state of dusk.

And I knew us just like this: like a night that forever greets an open field. And the weight of that darkness, which is no burden to the grass it lowers itself slowly over.

It was that summer we finally met, which is to say that we kept meeting, kept finding ourselves held in this endless arrival.

The Song of the North American Chiminey Swift

How else do I enter our story? I know only dust
devils and feathers to compare, an heirloom music
box missing several pins.

The motions of her pleated skirt, the gear-work
logic I thought with. A lid I saw lifted
from the field – its music and mirror

of pastures passing behind me.
If the melody was broken, it was only
the cracked silver-backed glass of our fault-

lined reality – a fall-out reason we found in all
the flickering lamps of our tavern-riddled town.
But we knew also the fields and the chimneys

across them. The chimney swifts circling
in clouds above us, like
a migratory mindset that would hold

in the sun-long evenings of that summer.
And I began to know her as my every
feathered thought. And then the feel

of my fingers dovetailing her ribs.
And then I knew only our pelvic
augury of song.

Allerton in Summer VI.

That lamp-scatter in the long view of those nights, up in the hillsides, in far off fields. A house now sprawled all over. A house the electrical glow tried to cull from that darkness.

The skyline and whiskey shared between us. And sometimes I thought you were a home within and at times a home that was without me.

Sometimes I babbled every silo in the country and the nights imagined a column of daylight still inside us.

Maybe I counted out all the tree lines I minded, something with which you could subtract the more distant horizons.

But this I remember: our affect was like no warming pattern I had known. A weather we felt would never be common or loveless. Like after you moved in, how we'd walk home from the bars and our talk was always some cordial storm.

Like when the evenings started to grow short and we kept slurring the most courteous summer.

Actaeon, to Diana

For a time my body took its curse as some beauty:
my storied poor foresight reset in socketed black moons,
all luster and pelted.

My stag's heart, its customs and cloven.

I felt how my body became mid-gallop –
a mess of legs lost to

adoration and bucking.

Felt my mind turn white and
clean as marble.

How my blood wanted
this marred bark trail: my torso

an earnest baggage – my desire as antlers
snagging in branches.

What beauty now bewildered,
I hope you will take my tattered velvet like love

letters littering the forest – my body
taking all the bruises I can offer –

here, take the heft of me lusting how you fabled.

§

Argus, All Your Eyes Are Sleeping

When the hundred eyes around your head are open,
Argus, your skull is mostly roof and floor, more archways than

walls, so the days move swiftly through you.
Or is your mind simply the place where you are? Maybe a loom

just as large? Your own pastoral. Yourself embroidered among cedars.
As in mine, is the river Inachus flooding the underground? Does

the run-off sewer-system fill with his worry? Argus, when showing
him his lost daughter – her words replaced with lowing,

her fair skin turned to rough hide that lowers his eyes –
does he know your own are lit with dim stars despite

the daytime outside? I know: the gods gave you a job so
you do it, you lead that poor calf to any pasture you think of. I know:

we're all wrong or being wronged. It's like in Mercury's song when
the gods turn some nymph to reeds to save her from Pan. But then

Pan just transforms her to pipes. Then he communes with her daily.
Argus, you would know all this, but Mercury

has just sung all your eyes to sleep. Still, I imagine your dreams
are of the gods and their tricks, but where does your mind go

when all your eyelids have closed? Juno, who looks deep into
the heart of you, says a thick mist has set up its darkness under the sun.

I don't know where she sits, Argus, but here the day is done.
Not quite light or dark but more an approaching night, and like

your eyes before they closed, the windows around town
flicker as though there are pale-blue stars inside.

Allerton in Autumn

Sentences in the Picturesque

The news as we know it is all township, an old
cobbled drama syndicated in pavement.

Watching our lifetime through windows
we rent, it's all new and easy, but if the fences

spell the ages, then the chain-link and picket yards are
an era we can walk away from –

the world we would rather all rough-hewn and possible.

So let us choose the measure of our plotlines – ambling
the dirt roads in daylong asides, let us forget

the subject of telephone poles, their hanging wires predicated;
instead, we should welcome the cadence of aging

barns, a clause-work of homesteads
we will own, and let us love like this one sentence

the whole autumn long – our affection in
the words of this season, in letters

that portrait this country. Maybe our wishes
will store in the farm wells for safe keeping,

in water that remembers like a mirror,
like the sentence longing for

the object that ends it. A scene we will
scan quickly over, until the cresecent moon

sinks into our evening, like some unwelcome comma,
to call us back home with its silence.

Allerton in Autumn I.

The summer repeated its green so long we had almost stopped listening. A word written wherever until, by August, all it stood for was a branchful of letters.

That color all about town, broad-stroked in the woods that were only a few green lights away. That forest we took back home in spare parts. Or maybe as pages torn from a storied wilderness once, to accent the retelling of today.

And I knew us just like this: like my spine had creased over this season, was a worn book you had taken to heart.

Like the scrawl inside me had become some almanac now that every myth had been fabled. But though the morning repeated you in the doorframe to the bathroom, the gestures you made yourself up with proved a vocabulary expansive and earnest.

That's something I long remembered – a greeting I found inside those moments you neared your departure.

So no surprises when, amidst the green everlasting, a red speck appeared. An orange speck, and a yellow, and a new season entering this world through its leaving.

No surprises when I saw a tree line flaming autumnal. When I saw a tree line on fire and sensed words I would still have to learn. A season's worth of scenery I had yet to tell you.

Instructions for Bewilder and Amend

for Bob and his boys

When father sets into a summer's open field
a cellar is the simplest answer.

When mother passes into the lamp-lit box that doorways
the bedroom – her bedtime story so quickly
a bygone – a darkness she now leaves behind her

And above your bed the full moon is
some bright sky above a well you rest in
For this you will find words and the someday they say

believe the night sky and its houses
arrive the seasons and believe they reopen

Believe: in your head a doorway will remain
to take you to the autumn where you found it
standing over a box they made dark as fresh dirt

Believe: the cellar where father would take
the shoes still unshod and believe the horses still there
still alive underneath the backyard

If another spring arrives and no doorway
keep your eyes on the ground – the crowns
of colts will soon split the sod – believe they will

rear right through

Allerton in Autumn II.

Maybe autumn was a procession of last breaths, what with each leaf's bright gasping. The colors loud for a season said hoarsely. No, the autumn wasn't so hard, so much as the sidewalk blocks I walked around this town could make up the longest calendar rows.

So much as I thought a country of tree lines on fire and saw the street lamps much closer.

Maybe some trees had yet to burn in early-autumn parks while the wide medians were still blushing with September's last flowers. But what else were those lit streets other than a farewell we took to the country – a wilderness we trafficked in a clockwork of dusk and dawn.

How else can I say it? Our lives were this small city when love turned into the everyday: ourselves held all quotidian in the streets, spoken like the autumn's small talk.

No eloquence needed to make sense of us. Nothing affected or pastoral. Nothing we renamed just to lie about it.

No. The autumn wasn't any hardship. It was only the season when the motor of each leaf seizes and rusts. Only a city and the several months of concrete that the trees' lost pages would crumble across.

A Manufactured Country

On our walk down the gravel shoulders, I wondered if
to the cars we were just figures in
the scenery, if to the scenery we stood for

more signs of the road and the cars
were moving right through us. Then she said
the barns looked like the faces of old

men she knows. And for
awhile I imagined my head held
her words in a light-slatted darkness.

But the rest of that day, I could think only of
our hewn meadow after
rough housing amidst bales of rolled hay.

Later, the ages just lay there while we watched
the clouds made
to billow from the mill. And I wondered if

the body was a green pasture inside. And I asked
if no one but the horizon remembers
where it's broken. No one

but the shift-change could answer, the parking lot
exhaling its cars
to the country. *Maybe the men*

in the train-yard, she said

long after. Like

a world bound in steel rails we would never escape.

Allerton in Autumn III.

And the horseshoes all rewoven as railways and speed.

And the last few blue skies this city could think of. The white line of a plane passing above like some scar I could hardly remember. No, nothing so much as the trains blurred the wilderness faceless.

Or so the country I could barely recall between myself and myself elsewhere, a distance that appeared only in the time-lapse on the schedule.

Or maybe a hallway was what the train lines made of the landscape. A syntax abridged between far off towns.

Or maybe I just hoped a world I was forgetting would keep ticking on. Like each hope was an engine block under the soil. Like the engine blocks would keep the fields running.

To Callisto, Who was First a Girl, Then a Bear, Then Later, The Bear Constellation

If I peel back the wallpaper of this world, Callisto, will I find
myself in your age? Will I be closer to you?

If the crows show as chips in a pale sky, does it mean
you still decorate the distance somewhere? I know that here

holds my face like a motel's portrait
hung in the lobby of each day. And the night's room

has curtains I can pull back to see if your slow gait in stars
still crosses my latest black window. You know, sometimes

I imagine us the sole cast in Arcady – the gods unwritten,
without us. And it is for spite that they spell our bodies

in animals, that they turn us to wonder
where we go beneath our coarse hides, our coats growing thicker

with each passing winter. And how your groves grow odious,
how my rooms in the city speak

as though they don't know me, as I walk the freshly painted halls
of each year. But if I were a bear, Callisto –

you amongst poplars, myself nearby the populace –
how I would tear through this world to companion.

Allerton in Autumn IV.

In parks and wooded lots, each tree was a lamp going out.
Each *light* a word crumbling. A word that once made you
think *warmth* and *lungs*. Both *lungs* and *bright*.

This park-thought we took in, knew it wasn't the wilderness
we wanted: the branches lacking fire; just charred wicks after
we blew out the candles in our apartment

And that apartment a once house. And the house an answer for
some forest no longer.

How a wick without flame looks empty. How the darkness
would rise from its chair in the corner, take our shadows
down from the wall.

A darkness like the fireplace that never worked, its grate full
with dead leaves.

Or a creak in the floorboards that said you couldn't sleep.
And that lonely rest you would locate in the medicine
cabinet, its mirrored doors you took as an exit out of your
pale portrait of grief.

And that other side a dark woods. A slumber you had only
to pluck from its branches. This was how the house dreamt you

asleep and safe in a forest it had once been.

They Apply Pigeons, to Draw Vapors from the Head

A mist will spill from any well in autumn, while the night sky
settles to shatter-water fallen across the lawn. Now this morning
tells only of you in footprints heading for the well.

So I usher you back to our sunless room – your fevered
brow beading with a dew all its own. There you recall
that physicians had once applied a pigeon to draw
vapors from the head.
                                        And now you imagine wings rising
from the damp field of your hair, their claws clung
to a sinuous mist swept from the meadows you think in.

If only the pigeon could draw a single ghost you thought of,
were there a single field in which your mother still stood. Instead,
a sickle-moon rests in your well-deep head, and tonight,
the atmosphere offers no bodies.

It's hardly mythology – the world thinking motherless
despite us, a pigeon still open-winged in a column of mist
now condensed to a circle of water.

Allerton in Autumn V.

And then we woke to a smokestack always. The morning's whole demeanor mechanical.

The weather systems repeating, redundant at my feet in the puddled-weeks coming. An overcast the airplanes had been lost to, so that I took their sound to be the nothing all over: like confusion, but how confusion means a thought you can't pull clean from the chaos of everything.

Or so a world awash in white-noise. A parent we lost further and further into the static of the telephone.

And maybe I just wanted the country to love us like distance allows. Like how you were, for a time, contented by the light pollution of your night-time medications.

Maybe I wondered how this ever-waning autumn got spent so quickly. Wondered why the wilderness kept me night-walking my sleep in our household, my dreamless fumbling at the doorknobs. And no rusted key in my hand by morning.

No rust-colored morning sky. No, the wilderness just left me omegas of dirt all over the hallways.

The Innocent Walk Blindfold Among Burning Plow-Shares without Being Scorched and Singed

Any father will teach you, where the plow quits
you let it rest forever.

Each fall you will burn the field, and after
the stubble is gone, the plowshares
will smolder well into November.

Over years they will sear
a constellation in the field, which becomes a night long
formed in your mind.

In time, your forehead will furrow and grow
nothing useful. So it's not enough, anymore,
to just plow through, but your tradition

of fetters, a folklore of whiskey
to blind you.

Stumbling in the fields, your throat
burning its autumn, you will come to recognize

the pale blue sky as your father's eyes
and your failure to figure
the stars behind them.

And Then One Day the Blue Sky Dims Starless

And then one day, the blue sky dims starless inside your skull,
which means the deepest slumber.

The last forests give to pining.
        The fields, for the last time, furrow while
they hide beneath blankets of concrete.

Through the smog-cover without you, hear
the satellites reshuffling above. It says:

                so much for the houses you thought in.

The keys and horseshoes you bury
        inside yourself, as though your body were a casket
and as though that casket were a question we had

answered together.

§

Taking the North Wind to Heart

In the age when I prayed to you, Orithiya, your body
sunned and sung itself to trees and each leaf
shimmered to greet you.

Know the time of their greenness
was measured by the distance I kept.

Then came a time when I drew near, and you went
uncertain as the boughs and fog that housed you.

In the cold I turned slowly the places you were,
and if I wanted delicacy, it was only my wanting

to love you clearly, to undress the foliage
that disguised you.

Despite myself, despite my back
braced against the heavens, my ever-pining in

your forest, your esteem aches with the pressure,
your knuckles go white and

crack like stones in this weather.
Know that this is what it means to let me in.

This is you learning my season.

Allerton in Winter

Allerton in Winter I.

Walking between two homes. We couldn't quite remember. The dimmer switch of autumn had revolved. The dimmer days always returning.

And their tungsten skeletons had cauterized each leaf alive. The trees like globes that had shattered one by one: a forest a flutter of bursting balloons.

And the overcast just then visible, just then closing like a small child's skull. And so the winter came as a thought we had entered and couldn't exit. The forest then further interiors, a picture of nerves stripped from the earth and covered in bark. That I can't forget. That I felt so passively and passing.

I never made the staircase you wanted, rising in a field to no story, in what house. I don't know why. I saw how the sun still touched the top branches. I just thought the darkness was all I could hold of your beauty.

Epitome

The winter arrives as no little gift.

The winter will never return
our gratitude. It sends back all

our thank you cards,
don't mention it illegible on the envelope.

I'm sure. Because it's winter when you walk
into a room and know
the window like a sentence left open.

Because the furnace inside us hums under the season,
won't hear of its silence.

Because I can feel the beams mutter under
the dead trees filling the attic,

its space a sheet we darkly
forest with words.

All down the street, the branches
scrawl the dormer windows.

I'm sure: the winter hardly notices.
It returns us every year
unread in our own white packet.

Allerton in Winter II.

And a white speck appeared. A white speck and another and a dark sky lighter with falling.

Soon the white sheets all over. The snow drifts like covered tables and couches some family had left for our winter. And we realized this world was always the remains of a mansion long since abandoned. Or so I

remembered the furniture left useless inside me. The birdcall where a wall once was but no longer. Only the cloud-cover was a ceiling that knew its height darkly. Only the echo of the birdcall a moment later.

And the trees were all doorways in profile. In one room, the forest was all darkness. Then I turned around and saw the moonlight rise from the white ground, haunting among the bare trees. And the field beyond was a large, empty chamber you took inside yourself. So I understood within you were thinking elsewhere.

I knew all your second-story doors were open. Knew I would find no stairway.

But maybe that darkness meant something. Like how our hands came undone and this whole place became us. This whole place a loneliness that was too big to hold in.

Writing Us in This Age and Its Climate

All winter, we amble about town like mowers lost when
the pastoral went missing.

In the bars we take tables for some expanse
we can manage, somewhere we can tend closer.

But here, each of us is a thing of shanks and wrists,
no more than a fiction of coats.

All winter you see through me, this place,
some past still here but no longer, which is all

irony but depressing and the smell of scorched wheat
from the factory affirms this.

These nights I respond remotely and you watch
an expanse gaining its snow.

I know, you don't love where we are, but what else
can I show you – the memories I held on to

are smooth stones gathered in my wrists,
gravel taken to my ankles.

I have learned no love comes
easy in this age, its climate. I know the production

of warmth is like any trade. I've learned that
it is nothing you apologize for.

Allerton in Winter III.

The snow fell outside our dark apartment. Fell and gathered. We watched it falling through a window in which our faces floated.

And we thought that somehow the landscape looked right through us. The snow that gathered falling into the part of us projected on to the exterior. Our white capes. An else of dark water.

And then a light flicked on. A light fell on and caught in the glass flashing to mirror. My image stamped over outside, but the light placed you elsewhere. I watched me in this window and barely saw you walk off into your distance, where the light failed to flesh you from the darkness (which calls to and gathers its distance).

That night like underwater. That night like some other house you walked into and became its dark windows.

The Vacated Season

When the off-white winter outside
matches our off-white painted walls, no longer

any windows. Or so a home
disguised in this distance.

You're late, again, for work, and the clock
like a blue moon hung in the top-right

corner of today. This hour's cracks
branching the plaster. As though trunks will

be found near the baseboards, the wood floor
buckling with their roots. As though

I am only a snow drift of white
covers on the bed when

you leave and the apartment
welcomes this vacated season.

Travelling from Home

The snow drifting whte erasure, like a map's margins
flooding the roads. The telephone poles
disguised as packet-boat masts,

each boat a question poorly buried, a question that left us
with no correspondence – nothing quite enough

for my mother's worried voice racing from gaff to gaff.
So I offer no answers, only that

I'm busy teaching the children of factory families to write
a new physics for furnaces and presses – not

the physics of irony, or of anger as it slowly
deepens into grief – they will lose them-

selves regardless. Example this town's five-
factory corners, the exhaustion effacing

the night sky – how I tell them, *go on, navigate.*
When my mother asks me how I'm doing,

I just ask her to send more Dramamine and ginger.
I talk her through the hours I watch the unused field

out the window, its barn like my only fixed spot in
a sea of white swells. I tell her how I can't figure

the question but I know from here I can't see
the factory further, except for a red light cresting

the smokestack. I tell her how the light flashes like
a dove's clamoring for amnesty, how that clamor

denotes a stark branchless.

Allerton in Winter IV.

Down the hallway, the branches creaked in the wind like old men looking for some lost thing. The white sheets just tried to let it rest. A thousand leaves were there and could barely work up a whisper.

But the tree-line reminded me of some distance – each snow-flake a small page that fell from a balcony. Like some forgotten fury haunting the absence it left inside us. It was something someone had said we will understand when we grow older.

And I knew us just like this: like our childhood homes were torn apart, were scattered across a world that was ever expanding.

The memories all under the white sheets. Each lonely tree from a forest ripped to pieces. Each farmhouse alone on the horizon like a story we assume will someday make sense.

Now that I'm older, I have only come to know my features as worn furniture awaiting the guests. Elsewhere your eyes, I imagine, are being turned down.

Elsewhere a tree-line that meant something once, but now I can't quite remember. Can't even imagine. And I just want to take it all back into myself. Like some forest of empty armchairs all pulled together.

Orpheus, to His Own Persephone

The Midwest admirably measures your absence.
My windshield frames this landscape where your presence voltas.
The mother, done searching, tucks me in her
grieving, wrings the warmth from her hands until winter
cracks the home water heater and piping. Then the nymphs fall to
pieces and stream deep through fissures to meet you.
My mind drifts to motor from the weather where it happens.
I can only find you in the window of your name, which locates
you in prairies not possible. My eyes follow the smokestacks to gather
the billow-down clouds that canopied our slumber.

The factory airs replace the underground, un-land lock populations.
Your presence in every location below this winter whitewashes
me completely. This is how I spill across several time zones,
tidal and thoughtless.

Allerton in Winter V.

And the winter spells us in a country so vacant it's a wonder the crossbeams of our bodies don't buckle.

I know: all the families are elsewhere. And we hadn't any notion of ghosts. We had no idea of our haunting. Or how the roofless silos hold, just like us, a column of gust and flurry inside them.

And all we have left is this game that we play where we are missing. Where I watch every drift of snow like white covers that might tell of your breathing.

This is how your call pulls me to every possible departure. Your absence spelling everywhere in white. The up tucked down. The river frozen over. You hide with your reasons. I have never said another or goodbye.

And here's what I believe to be true: we have long since grown up but we are still walking inside the mind of a child. So sometimes I just think my legs in your bed to see how that feels. I sometimes sink my legs in your bed and go on floating at night. Your white light sailing me somewhere.

And you are all the places I fear I'll forget when I'm older. So I'm loving everywhere to find out how you feel: my torso bobbing about you, my heart bobbing in me as in the silo where you accumulate as snow.

A Crosshatch of Rising Cinders, Falling Snow

All fires require rekindling—
regardless of whether

we've built ourselves hearthless.

Poor doorstep. The deadbolt and handle

lie in a threshold's ashes
my shoes now divulge to the snow.

Flurries in the lamplight push
this way, now that. What tracks

don't adore themselves,
adore their tautology

to nothing? I'm holding
patterns circling home

—my cabin

fever and axes.

Orpheus, to No One but Himself

From here, the moon is a manhole to streets
we climb toward – its cover coming crescent,

the crescent waning closed.
Then your hand tightens in mine. Your silence says

my name and turns me to absence.
But walking this town's dark where you aren't, the pressure

in my palm isn't nothing, nor ceasing.
By morning, the feel of your fingers flickers to blackbirds,

makes for the thickets. All day their flurry
of quarter-rests crochets in the park, inaugurates

your auspices I gather. Eurydice, my eyes play your flocks
recoded in the coppice while the dark blue shades

assemble about me – a pell-mell of poplars and lampposts,
old-brick apartment shaped shadows.

My mouth opens to call you and a bitter river
just rolls out. So I seethe about town. My head spills you all over

again. I bellow your name to the gutters, the sewers
murmuring wherefore, all throughout the underground.

I try to float you here, and in the underwater blur
the trees nearly pull you off, but you abash

too easy when I near you. You return to abandon,
and my darling, when I call you, I need you to come closer,

no matter how uncertain your skin.
I'm headed off all drifted and orphaned, and I know

this song only carries me elsewhere,
its notes will only displace you.

I know my head is all feverish winter;
it's a northwest passage I am trying to break through.

§

To Alcyone, from Your Dead Husband

Behind my face the ship was already in the slipway,
a turbulent sea unfurled in my thinking. But my eyes held

still before you, like a curtain embroidered with your country.

The aftermath will be painful, I imagine: your delicate

sewing of my lips, those lines you will offer for
my last words; the warp of my body and my warmth

like red threads already unwoven. If you look inside me,

you will find only shipwreck and cold ocean, nothing of
where you waited. All I can say is that the body, like any vessel,

has no choice in its tenor, that despair is water poured, bail
by bail, back into an ocean of water.

But know also the vessel will shape what it holds.
Or so my body was a spool that had been empty

with wanting, that tried to rewind its loss
in fathoms of blue thread to find you.

Allerton in Spring

Allerton in Spring I.

Spring was a memory this town struggled to recall. The same old grass and snow argument hashed out on every lawn.

Something you look at and say: *only the bad habits come easy.* And know stubbornness a ready answer. How we never forgot our cold-shoulder go to.

This much is certain: the ungodly gray slush by the streets wanted only the gutters.

And all you could remember of this winter was a crescent moon's constant presence near your head. A prescripted ease with which you had forgotten each evening's destruction. That sliver-spill of stars across your sleep.

Or maybe you learned that growth meant forgetting. Maybe the winter was something we just had to swallow. And now I understand how you saw it, on your drives out passed the town limits: the fields flanking with a crosshatch of stubble emerging, their promise of return all moonlit.

But those days I saw only the muddy husk of the past year. The moonlight and stubble a static pasture on the television set back home.

The fields humming their poor reception. A question about my waxing or waning resolution.

And I thought the winter and its song would go on forever inside us. And I recalled the liquor bottle jostle in your backpack as you would climb the stairs to our apartment, how the bottles would sing their glint when shattered.

I didn't want to say it, but I couldn't stop thinking this winter had been beautiful: the landscape all snow and broken glass.

Maybe what you heard, I could not: a goodbye hidden inside the spring's arrival. Like the winter's slow runoff in the sewers. Its low but hopeful murmur. Its long, sleepy call to the river.

Another Evening at the Abandoned Fairground

We sat and smoked cigarettes in the bumper cars wanting
contact, electricity.
Later, side-saddled on our own frozen gallop,

we watched the landscape in the dim mirrors of the carousel,
which looked just as blighted as it does
out the bottom of empty glass bottles.

That night we remembered a meadow was
under the fairground. So we lay down to watch the sky
and could imagine no better reflection.

We believed each star was a plowshare on fire,
that our plastic horses were tilling
this place with flames.

A Process Called Night and Rain

The night has its own machinery. The mind
when dreaming is built from its model.

Like the bare branches I saw as a darkness scribbled across
a moonless sky. The rain reconfigured in the trees.

The rain inside me and the rain outside the room –
one is mixed with your breathing, which is too heavy

and tells me the trouble of our sleep. In one I look up
at a window and know the dark where we are,

a sky that rises and falls like a chest.
I know the rain outside us, and I know the water on

the wood floor, the wall's shimmering rivulets. Inside,
I wake up and realize a night storm is working through

its process, the roof is leaking, that we are well into our last
year in this house. For hours, the ceiling like a puddle

of night while the rain offers what sense
can be made of us, these days. The ground we know,

like the body, is an engine wanting water.
In a year this house will be torn down, and the night has

a gear-work we can learn even if the mechanical whirl
of our worry won't listen. When the lights in all

the brass fixtures dim. When they drip with centuries of water.
The rot in the mantle all beaux-arts and useless. In a year

we will sleep somewhere else. When we wake in the morning,
the ground will have swallowed a whole night of rain.

Allerton in Spring II.

What could we make of winter's unravel, those days wall-papered with rain and fog.

The granaries all emptiness and echo. Wonder the engines lost to the fields. Wondered what harvest was next.

It was difficult, the wanting of tenderness then. The tending. The branches budding over last year's leaves turned to dregs in the gutters. A strange dialogue after a winter of silence.

And I didn't know where we stood. Or so I kept turning *unravel* over in my mouth. Wondered the world this green cemetery. Unravel. Redress. Unravel. Wonder the world this green.

Like some ground between wrecked and majestic. Just like us. A wilderness between undressed and sparkplugged.

Wondered what to say next in moments we just stood there, our hearts poor gadgets in each other's hands. Those days, every thought of you awoke, tinkered about itself like something that wanted fixing.

And maybe I imagined us still forged in our bed then, the bulbs rising from that soil.

Maybe I imagined a tungsten glow all over.

To Pomona, in a House in Pomona, California

Is your love built in electric grids you think
or idylls you believe to still be in the heartland?

The deer you saw this morning through a window
to your yard, is it your sylvan wish refrained, or is

the hart, now bounding down the street,
some error in the loaded

fog of this dawn?

Baucis & Philemon

With each sob, crows are flown from her rib cage, filling the room
with their clamor. I've chased helpless, clipped-winged geese around us
for days. They find the counterpane to hide behind and vanish.
If only we could offer ourselves to oblivion. But the gods shake

their heads and refill our glasses, the wine bottle still
full and begging disbelief. The kettle calls and glows its red warning,
but I keep pulling twigs from the walls and roof for kindling
until fire consumes the home we had made in this hovel.

So the gods walk us to high ground, where the gravel path proves
difficult to grovel on. With each step ascending, water fills
a valley we walk away from, laps at our ankles.

And the gods only offer our bodies to oblivion. And the nightingales
now flutter from the folds of Baucis's clothes, while the missing
geese float calm as swans on the lake swelling behind us.

Then a ship coalesces and only requires the wind's breath. Its berth
rolls out the water like bells tolling: the village drowning in its sound.
For days the gods cast us to night on this dark mirror, which
makes two black skies we bob between. Here, Baucis lies in

my arms and dreams, the birds cooing softly in her torso.
When the lake eventually rises to the firmament, we lay pinned
between the boat and this ceiling. The small hull corrodes
into soil, becomes a burial mound we can climb through.

Our legs root to the floor, band into trunks while the bark
takes our bodies. The boughs our limbs stretch to achieve, and then
the sudden bird-scatter of our heads clearing, as a last thought buds
about mingled fingers. As our minds condense and then cork.

Long after, a knotted greenery remains and muses. The two trunks
pillar an aria of bird calls that means *dear,*

companion.

Allerton in Spring III.

And a green speck appeared. A green speck and another and the trees unfolding a color that had long slept inside them.

A color that meant desire slowly disclosing. The fault lines of parking lots and sidewalks erotic with grass and weeds.

Or so that feeling had been budding about us for weeks. And I wanted you to see the brickwork relearning its ivy. The concrete lots sinking back into the soil.

I wanted to show you the white sign with its blue crown, which had once stood before a gas station and then it stood for the station no longer. A sign that watched the slow story of this meadow's return.

I wanted you to see the white sign like a memory glowing somewhere inside us. Like a square cut out of the darkening sky. A blue crown suspended there all kingdom, a kingdom all absence and abundance beyond.

A window hung over this bewilder of asphalt and pasture. A scene that, each evening, the gloaming held together.

And that empty lot I wanted you to know as devotion, its lush exhaustion of dusk. Because the foliage fills out this world but also obscures it. Because we forget everything was already ruined, and what the ruins can give.

Because I couldn't locate where I loved you then. I just knew this was how it looked.

Hamlet, Indiana

Not all our madness is lovesick: after all we have
this sinking Denmark to contend with;
here our depression is only the town's depression
lacking romance – nobody drowns
themselves in the river, no one would be
caught dead there.

And it's not depressing depending
on how we embrace it: we have our crumbling Victorians,
our easy afternoons cheering the ivy,
knowing how this ends.

No, it's not depression when you embrace me, lying on
the cold wood floor, staring up at the water stained ceiling,
at the chandelier with its ornaments
long fallen, a couple bulbs
still working.

The Once Watauga Valley

The flood, she might have said, was worth loving.

Or maybe: look at the rising water, its perfectly
flat field, and what that does with
the height of the silo.

Or she said nothing, but her eyes
shined on their color – a gold-green prairie
learning a blue-green current.

And where the trail had washed out, she swam
across it. And when I followed I thought
of the town below Watauga Lake, in the once
Watauga Valley.

I imagined as we floated the clumsy ascension
of pews in the church hall,
the furniture castaways in their lost living rooms.

Imagined the town stood there, at first
oblivious as its second stories. As gables
all vacant-faced on a summer day.

Thought the portraits drifting
out the windows. The amnesia in
the wallpaper peeling.

But I can't forget how her eyes blurred
into the flooded field around her,
like a well filled and surrounded with water.

And all at once I felt the cascades over
the sills of the town's dormer windows,
and she said then: *see what the river*

does with the silo, the emptiness it was
holding inside.

Allerton in Spring IV.

Or so a light flicked on in our minds. A spring's dawn-light filling a bedroom. A brightness you swallow or sing.

A light falling on us caught in our bodies, the entwining of so many landscapes. Those days spent with our palms against this soil, mapping the pulse where it returned.

And this I knew: the place we were, or had been, would stand monument for nothing, would exhibit only the world we took in and thought toward. The days of fertile pastures, the fallow. The oceans of corn before a stubble-field distance.

The summer that soon shuts down, has only its dim death to offer the turned back of autumn.

Or so a snow filled silo stands only a few months away from a well full with clear water. Elsewhere a December granary replete with August. A grocery store that closed one October and now its parking lot fills only with May prairie.

Now plywood boards over the store's blind windows, and I watch the finger and the ghost you trace across them.

I see you recall a forest we once were. I watch you smile as your eyes fall on me and replace this season in my throat.

A Letter from Pythagoras

I have seen myself the firm fields
filling with sea, the sea outgrowing
the tree lines hemmed on the mountainsides.

We salvage where we can so I turn
the plow to an anchor and hope it will fasten.
And we must forgive the valley, which will not

hold either. Say goodbye to our lost topography,
its persistence. A letter I will write for
the vessel, which begins with its last departure and ends

with its opening address. And the wax seal
stamped with an anchor will only be broken.
It's fine. The epigram will say on our behalf: *a vessel means*

nothing with no port to steer toward. At least something
will be made of our loose strands.
Or so I have written to tell you the heart,

like any vessel, is no more than its small relief.
It says nothing of inside. It's only
what we break when we want

within us. And so we break
endlessly. And so we learn there is nothing, not
even ourselves, that can hold us apart or together.

Allerton in Spring V.

Behind our apartment, the forested lot keeps growing into more forest. A distance reminding itself with trees and trees.

In the canopy, a hundred crows shuffle, resettle. Between two homes we walk and are a thought recomposing in each other.

And maybe the lot wasn't vacant so much as a house without people or walls. So blessed be the lonely armchair still out there. Blessed the dinner table dumped last year and now holds only the weather. A past kept, a past now claw-feet deep in the soil.

Like a rusted car all godless in a thriving thicket. Like a suitcase holding our lives had expanded until its clasp finally broke. That's how the story that was ever our meanwhile went. Like each room was a memory we could waltz into or out of.

Each tree a doorway in profile and each one crowned with a horseshoe.

And maybe forgiveness was in every horseshoe we buried, the skeleton keys they became. *Because*, you said, *the summer will be worth reopening*. Because a sign lit up in the clearing was a white square to unlock the blue-black night.

Because for so long I thought of you as a home where I wasn't. And myself made sense only as some lone house inside its single-tree horizon. But here the forest overgrowing every room since. Here the branches I feel break and bloom through all the blind windows that façade me.

Acknowledgements

I wish to thank my parents and sister for their love and support, as well as for the understanding that they have always shown me.

I would like to express a deep gratittude to Brigit Kelly, Graham Foust, and Brenda Hillman – without you I would not have believed poetry could still matter, nor that I could write it well enough. I would also like to thank Michael Palmer, Norma Cole, and Joyelle McSweeney for their guidance at the early stages of this project's development.

My thanks to Ryo and Lily, who have been true comrades in poetry.

Thanks to the St. Mary's MFA program and to my workshop compatriots. Thanks also to Purdue University's English Program and its faculty for continuing my education in poetics and its place in the world.

I would also like to thank the editors and staff at the following journals, where some of these poems have previously appeared:

American Poetry Journal: "Orpheus, to His Own Persephone" (previously titled "Plucked") and "Baucis & Philemon." *Barrow Street*: "A Crosshatch of Rising Cinders, Falling Snow." *Copper Nickel*: "No Narrative," "Blót," "A Manufactured Country," "Allerton in Winter II," "Allerton in Winter IV," and "Allerton in Winter V." *Denver Quarterly*: "Allerton in Winter [I]" and "Allerton in Winter [III]." *Dislocate*: "A Legend of Loose Brick Children" (previously titled "Western Union Discontinues the Telegraph"). *Handsome*: "Travelling From Home" and "Hamlet, Indiana." *Hayden's Ferry Review*: "Narcissus and Echo, Two Voltas, a Field of Illinois" (previously titled "Notes on Plaines"). *Nimrod*: "The Song of the North American Chimney Swift" (previously titled "Transphysical"). *Notre Dame Review*: "Our Apocryphal Chapter of Animals" and "Sentences in the Picturesque" *Real Poetik*: "To Callisto the Bear, Who Was First a Girl, then a Bear, then Later the Bear Constellation." *Verse Daily*: republished "No Narrative" and "Blot"

About the Author

A.E. Watkins is a graduate of the St. Mary's College of California MFA Program and currently attends Purdue University, where he is pursuing a Ph.D. in nineteenth-century British literature. *Dear, Companion,* his first collection of poetry, was runner up for the 2011 *Amercian Poetry Journal* Book Prize. His poems and reviews have appeared in *Barrow Street, Copper Nickel, Denver Quarterly, Hayden's Ferry Review, Ninth Letter, Sycamore Review,* and elsewhere.

www.ingramcontent.com/pod-product-compliance
Lightning Source LLC
Chambersburg PA
CBHW021508090426
42739CB00007B/521